CHAI

01 BECOMING A PERSONAL SHOPPER

BECOMING A PERSONAL SHOPPER

Love to shop? Would you like to get paid to shop for others? Let's turn that passion into a career and become a professional personal shopper. Personal shopping is often referred to as a dream job for many fashionistas. After 10 years as a full time personal shopper I know that you can create a business for yourself. It's lots of fun and most of all its very rewarding. Not only will you love going to work everyday, but your clients will also love what you do for them as well.

When deciding to become a personal shopper, you need to decide if you want to work for a high end department store or as an independent personal shopper. Many personal shoppers are located in large department stores. They will only buy and recommend to clients the clothes and accessories that are sold in that store.

As an independent personal shopper, you can offer a wide selection of clothing as you can buy from where ever you like - from the smallest boutique to the largest department store. This is a benefit that should be pointed out to your clients.

While there are no specific requirements in becoming a personal shopper, there are some areas of other employment you may consider before becoming a personal shopper. These include such areas as styling, marketing and working in fashion retail all of which can help you achieve your goal.

This personal shopping guide will give you the resources and ideas you need to succeed in the exciting world of personal shopping.

WHAT DOES IT TAKE TO BE A PERSONAL SHOPPER?

A fantastic personality, confidence AND someone who understands how to dress other people! As a personal stylist it is important to see the inner beauty of people and never 'judge a book by its cover'. A client may look or behave in a certain manner however their behaviour may hide an inner lack of confidence and a real need for help and advice. Working as a personal shopper transforms people's lives.

THINGS YOU WILL NEED:

- Address Book
- Electronic Personal Organiser
- Fashion Magazines

Get some experience; retail sales will give you a great foundation. You'll be in touch with products, trends, brand names and price points. Analyze the trends and develop your own ideas about how they can be worked into a man's or a woman's wardrobe.

Get written testimonials from your friends and colleagues about how much they value your ideas and trust your skills.
Start with colleagues from your previous profession, friends, relatives and neighbours.

As a personal shopper the advice you give to your clients needs to be as specific as possible. Compiling a list of do's and don'ts is also important. For example, your client may love the colour orange however during your consultation you have identified this as a colour that doesn't work for them. If you do not specifically address this, your client may well continue to buy in that colour. They will reason that as it has not been listed to avoid, they can still wear it.

You need to make clear everything they should avoid, particularly if they love it, otherwise it will be easy for them to slip into their old ways and lapse into something familiar. Create information sheets which will record your client's details, and add these into your own client database for future reference.Show your clients the correct colours to wear so as to best accentuate their features, save them time when shopping and stop them buying the incorrect colours.

Have a good understanding of hair shapes, colour and styling skills. Be very mindful when your client is getting changed. Do not enter a changing room unannounced.

Have very good knowledge of how to apply makeup. Makeup should be fresh and easy to apply for your client; your client needs to learn from you how to change her look from day into night. Provide your client with the essential tools of face charts and makeup images.

Working alongside your clients, giving advice at the right time and building their knowledge, will result in a client who is more confident in themselves.

WHAT IS A PERSONAL SHOPPER?

A personal shopper puts garments together, knowing what someone else will like, what they can wear and what will make them look and feel fantastic.

The personal shopping experience begins with an interview to determine a client's needs. It is recommended to conduct a colour analysis to ensure you and your client understands what colours and what season they belong to. This means that it is essential that you learn how to do colours.

As a personal shopper you will advise your client about certain brands, colours and other wardrobe tips. Some clients may choose not to purchase any products on the day. They may simply want your shopping advice and ideas for the future.

You, as the personal shopper, will take your client on a shopping expedition to fashion retailers in shopping malls, department stores, outlet stores and fashion boutiques.

Some personal shoppers do the shopping without their client; this means that you will deliver the suggested garments to the client's home or office for a private fitting. You will need to 'appro' the clothing or have the product put through on a credit card to secure the retailer's clothing. It is important to create good business relationships with retailers - this will enhance your personal shopping service.

WHAT DO YOU KNOW ABOUT YOURSELF?

As a personal shopper you must be well aware of current trends and what's happening in the fashion industry.
Here are some questions to think about.

- What are your thoughts about new trends? Do you followthem?

- How often do you change your hair style?

- Do you think you are creative?

- Do you play dress up in your own wardrobe?

- What are your interpersonal skills like?

- How do you feel about working with difficult people?

- What are your thoughts around makeup?

- Is skin care important to you?

- How do you like taking compliments?

- How do you stay up to date?

IMPORTANT QUESTIONS TO ASK YOUR CLIENT

The most important thing is to start talking to your client. Choose your initial questions carefully and find out what they want to achieve. Some questions need to be very direct and clear, although be aware that your client may not be able to answer you so clearly.

QUESTIONS TO ASK YOUR CLIENT:

- What is their shopping budget?

- Where do they usually shop?

- What do they think is missing in their wardrobe?

- What precisely are they unhappy with?

- How would they describe themselves as a person?

- How would they like to look?

Questions such as these will help you determine what your client's goals are. Be aware that people often want to revamp their look as the result of a personal change in their life. It's important to be mindful of the questions you ask. You certainly don't want to give your client the impression that you are prying into their personal life. It's important to keep all the information shared between you and your client confidential. You need to stay professional at all times.

Know your client's budget and respect it. Always offer your clients a variety of options, but avoid exceeding their budgets. You'll establish a bond and trust with your clients and keep them coming back for your services.

Ask your client for a detailed explanation of the look that they want to achieve. When you work with a personal shopper, she needs to know as much about you as possible before shopping. Ask your client what she does for a living and how she spends her leisure time. A stay-at-home mum can't be expected to wear heels and suits every day, so keep these things in mind when shopping. Ask your client to speak up, but listen too. Learning to work as a personal shopper can be difficult for some, because you have to learn how to balance your own opinions with those of someone elses.
If you pick out something that your client doesn't like, you need to be able to pick up that they don't like it. If there's something that your client isn't sure about, hear her out and gently encourage her to try it on. Your client may find that this is the one piece they love the most in the end. Working as a personal shopper can be an eye-opening experience if your client lets you do your job.

Diversify your offerings. Give your clients the option of using your services for corporate or family gift giving. Target Christmas and other special dates for gift vouchers well in advance.

"Fashion fades,
only style remains the same"
- Coco Chanel

WHAT YOU NEED TO KNOW AS A PERSONAL SHOPPER

As a personal shopping stylist it's very important to know your products and your brands. You will need to do your homework at the beginning of each season to ensure you know where the best buys are and what new brands have come into the market. Clients are buying your time so you must understand your client's needs.

IT'S IMPORTANT THAT YOU HAVE THE FOLLOWING SKILLS:

- A relaxed attitude

- A polished appearance

- Good punctuality

- A knowledge of the latest fashion trends

- Respect for your client

- A consistently professional demeanor

COMMUNICATION SKILLS

Good communication skills are key in projecting a good image. You may look good but speaking is also part of the image. Good communication skills can be learned. Self-esteem is tied to a person's communication skills. The more confidence a person has, the more likely they are to have effective communication skills. A person who lacks self-esteem will have a harder time communicating effectively with others.

Work with your client on their communication skills. After your initial conversation with them you should be able to notice any areas that need improvement. The first step in your client acquiring good communication skills is for them to become aware of how they are perceived. By understanding their own way of communicating with others, they will be able to better address any changes that need to be made.

One way of communicating more effectively with others is to mirror the style of others' communication. This makes the other person more comfortable with you.

A CLIENT'S ENQUIRY

Let's imagine you have advertised your services as a personal shopper. The phone rings and a potential client is on the line. They have seen your website or advertisement and want to know about your services. They will start by saying something like: "I saw your advert about personal shopping, I am interested in knowing a little more about your service". Your task is to engage the prospect in conversation. Concentrate on the prospect. Ask them:

Their name - make sure you have a notepad and pen by the telephone. It appears unprofessional if you take several minutes to find one.

"What is your situation?" or "How can I help you"? You need to encourage them to open up about themselves. Listen for the clue that tells you the client's problem. They may say: "I have a job interview and I don't know what to wear" or "I've recently divorced and would like to meet someone new".

This is when you say that you can help them. Tell the caller "it's important to look and feel good" and that you can certainly help.

TOPICS TO DISCUSS WHEN YOU MEET YOUR CLIENT

- Body measurements

- Preferred brands

- What fabrics they like and dislike to wear

- What colours they like and dislike to wear

- Presentation skills

- Grooming skills

- Self esteem

- Makeup

- Hair styling, colours and styles

- What to wear and what not to wear

- Underwear

- Colour

- Styling tips

- Overall image

CREATING A NEW IMAGE

Some clients may be daunted by the thought of changing everything at once. They may not be able to afford the money or time to renew their entire wardrobe etc. You will need to make them aware that such changes can be accomplished gradually.

It will be a help to the hesitant client if you can identify one key piece to set the change process in motion. This key piece could be related to their wardrobe or picking out new make up colours that will make a difference. From there, you can teach your client the art of gradually changing items over time, as and when their existing items need renewing and when their budget allows.

HERE ARE THE TIPS AND GUIDELINES YOU CAN PASS ON AT THIS STAGE:

- Note the one piece that will make the biggest difference to their wardrobe. Buy different makeup colours when needed.

- Make sure friends and family know what they are aiming for so that they can consider buying the right items for birthdays etc.

- Think twice before buying anything on sale.

- Take it slowly if they are nervous.

- Tell them to enjoy their new look and image!

PERSONAL SHOPPING AND WARDROBE PLANNING
You need to access your clients spending power, you can then help them make the most of the clothing budget. On the other hand, you may need to tactfully suggest they need to spend slightly more; you pay for quality.

Over-spenders may well come to you for advice because they spend a fortune but never seem to have anything to wear. Their purchases may be unwise or bought on impulse and based on emotional spending.

You can help these clients to spend less by purchasing clothes and accessories that really suit them. That way they will not 'fritter' their money away on one-off or sale items. Such purchases often do not go with anything else in the wardrobe.

New Zealand women spend around 10% of their income on clothing.

FURTHER SESSIONS AND CONTACTS WITH YOUR CLIENT

You can help ease your client into their new image by ensuring that they understand they are not alone. You are there to help them. Make sure your client is aware that you will be in touch, over the coming months, as they start to accept and move forward with their new image.

PERSONAL SHOPPING GUIDELINES

BASE COLOURS

Most wardrobes will have at least one or two base colours running throughout. These should be neutral colours such as black, brown, navy or grey.

QUALITY VERSUS FAST FASHION

Of course, most people tend to be on a tight budget and this should always be taken into consideration. However, there are a few items on which it is always worth spending a little extra.

A plain, tailored suit (for professional clients), a classic style pair of quality work shoes and a dateless, quality coat or jacket are all well worth the investment.

ACCESSORIES

No matter how great the outfit, it will somehow look incomplete without the necessary accessories. By adding a belt, bag, scarf or jewellery you can really complete an outfit.

SHOPPING CHECKLIST

Before your client makes a purchase, you need to be assured that your client has considered the following.

USE THIS AS A CHECK LIST:

- Did your client try the garment on? **This is a must!**

- Did you check the fit in the front and the back?

- Is the suit jacket long enough to cover the bottom?

- Are the button holes sewn tightly?

- Can your client move freely in the garment?

- Does the item feel comfortable? Check for pulls, bulges or bunching of the material.

- Does your client love the item?

- Ask your client why they like it.

- Does the garment work with the other pieces in the wardrobe?

- Always think - Clothes should look and feel fantastic.

"For beautiful eyes, look for the good in others; for beautiful lips, speak only words of kindness; and for poise, walk with the knowledge that you are never alone." - Audrey Hepburn

03 THE BUSINESS

HOW TO HAVE A SUCCESSFUL PERSONAL SHOPPING TRIP?
Make a list of everything you need or want a day or two before you go shopping. If you need shirts or pants, skirts, dresses or shoes, write it down. Keep a very careful list so you know exactly what you're looking for.

Get ready for the trip. Take a shower, do your hair and put on an outfit you look nice and feel comfortable in. Wear shoes that are easy to slip into and slip out of. Going into the trip feeling good about yourself will help make it more successful, and will keep you from being discouraged about the small things that escalate quickly.

Hire the best personal shopper you can find - someone who has lots of experience, someone you trust, and someone who has a good sense of style and who will tell you the truth.

Try on everything. This is the single most important rule of shopping: Try it on. You never know what something looks like until you've seen it on you. It doesn't look the same way on the mannequin or the hanger as it does on you. Just because you don't like something on the hanger doesn't mean it won't look good on you-and just because you do like something on the hanger doesn't mean it will look good on you.

Look in a 3-way mirror if you can and take the advice of your stylist. Don't purchase it unless you absolutely love it.

BOOSTING YOUR CLIENT

Everyone has a best feature. Emphasising this feature will boost your client's confidence, show off their personal style and enhance their overall image.

Facial features can be shown off with hairstyles, earrings, scarves and tops, all of which draw the eye upward. Collared tops can frame and flatter a great face and hide an aging neck line.

Women can also enhance facial features with makeup. Great lashes enhance gorgeous eyes and well-shaped eyebrows will, most importantly, create the overall frame of your face.

Great legs can be shown off in short skirts and dresses, high heels or even skinny jeans. Higher heels have the ability to flatter any size or shape leg, which is why they have been a wardrobe staple for women throughout the years.

Men can enhance a great upper body with fabrics that lightly hug the torso without being too tight.

Women can show off a great cleavage with just a peek of skin, for example through wearing a lace camisole peeking from beneath a top or jacket, or a boat-neck styled top.

Brighter colours will always draw attention and will always show confidence.

PROMOTING YOUR PERSONAL SHOPPING BUSINESS

Promoting your personal shopping business requires printing business cards which feature your services.

Word of mouth will be your best promotion. Using a PR company will certainly help promote your new business.
Local newspaper advertising is also an avenue of promoting your personal shopper business.
At certain times of the year you could target certain events i.e.
Weddings - Helping brides look for gifts for her wedding party by putting your business cards in local bridal boutiques.
Mother's day promotion - help the husbands find the perfect present.
Races - Shopping with men and women to find the perfect race day outfit.
Starting a personal shopper business can be a rewarding and exciting way to earn a living. Find your niche in what you like to shop for, get fliers and business cards made and start promoting your endeavour. Find out what other people are charging in the industry. This will give you and indication of the market rate. Look online and make some phone calls to those already in the industry.

FEES AS A PERSONAL SHOPPER

The amount you charge your client should be what you consider is worth your time and effort.

As you gain recognition as a personal shopper, your fee can increase substantially. Personal shoppers set their own rates, either hourly or a flat fee. When personal shoppers work in department stores, they are paid an hourly rate, depending on experience.

Personal shoppers can also go on to become stylists as they gain recognition. Celebrities call on stylists and personal shoppers to keep them up-to-date and in style.

TESTIMONIALS

"Just a quick thank you for a fun day out on Tues. I learnt so much and am inspired to look outside the square now. The sheep didn't recognise me when I got home.Thanks for making me feel at ease,you truly have a gift.Thank goodness for people like you, for the first time I actually wanted to stay in a clothes shop longer than 5 mins". Tania

"Just wanted to thank you again for last Wednesday. Even though I was WAY out of my comfort zone I had a great time. Andrew loved all the clothes and even told me to go and buy the expensive boots! I had my black dress on yesterday and loved it. I have been out shopping since and felt much more confident - I have now got the bug! My friends and family have all admired my new clothes, which feels great - my sister-in-law is especially inspired". Julie

"Thanks so much for your time. I had an absolute blast and learnt so much from you in such a short space of time. It is definitely money well spent and while many people would probably say they would never do it, they don't know what they are missing. The feelings of knowing you look good and can put an outfit together and have it work from head to toe is amazing". Sharlane

HOW TO BECOME A PERSONAL SHOPPER.

BY FASHION STYLIST
ANGELA STONE

Personal Shopping is a fabulous career that allows you to shop and help others create the look they
have always wanted. Angela Stone will show you how to create your own personal shopping business.

Made in the USA
Coppell, TX
15 January 2020